THE
TYPEWRITER
REVOLUTION

THE
TYPEWRITER
REVOLUTION & OTHER POEMS

by

D. J. Enright

THE LIBRARY PRESS
New York
1971

©*1971 by D. J. Enright*

International Standard Book Number:
0-912050-07-1

Library of Congress Catalog Card Number:
73-158612

Printed in the United States of America

CONTENTS

The Typewriter Revolution

THE LAUGHING HYENA

BREAD RATHER THAN BLOSSOMS

SOME MEN ARE BROTHERS

ADDICTIONS

THE OLD ADAM

UNLAWFUL ASSEMBLY

NEW POEMS

THE TYPEWRITER REVOLUTION

The typeriter is crating
A revlootion in peotry
Pishing back the frontears
And apening up fresh feels
Unherd of by Done or Bleak

Mine is a Swetish Maid
Called FACIT
Others are OLIMPYA or ARUSTOCART
RAMINTONG or LOLITEVVI

TAB e or not TAB e
i.e. the ?
Tygirl tygirl burning bride
Y, this is L
Nor-my-outfit
Anywan can od it
U 2 can b a
Tepot

C! *** stares and /// strips
Cloaca nd † -
Farty-far keys to suckcess!
A banus of +% for all futre peots!!
LSD & $$$

The trypewiter is cretin
A revultion in peotry
" "All nem r =" "
O how they £ away
@ UNDERWORDS and ALLIWETTIS
Without a.

FACIT cry I!!!

THE LAUGHING HYENA

(Birmingham, Egypt)

SWAN VILLAGE

(Birmingham—Wolverhampton New Road)

Did it turn out a goose? Did some loose
               liver,
Teetering homewards, run into a sheet?
Or was it some conurban Bernadette, who met
That white display of where the road would never
               stray,
That dizzy image, never quite forgotten by the
               busy village?

Or did some fierce and backward god, mad
For a female hand, land with lashing feathers
               and,
Finding Lemnos but no Leda, leave a
Noun generic to a dismal field, a file of houses,
               and a derrick?

Or, once upon a time, were swans upon a lake
— Like snowflakes on a silver ladle —
Able to evade the falling smuts,
               the avid poacher?
And is the 'Hen and Chickens' heir
               to the singing last sung there?

               Or is the bus conductor's cry
No real contention, just a clerical convention?

BLACK COUNTRY WOMEN

Did they burn in their men's furnaces —
              old women
Whose tired hair coils like cowed and
              dropping smoke,
All shades of grey about their burnt-out skulls?

Small deities of coal, who from your beds
              brought miners —
A narrow street now holds life's remnant,
              and your grey net bags:
You huddle evenings round your fires, each
Boss of a blackened little house.

Perpetual autumn grips this landscape:
              its chopped fields ever dying.
But spring unending flames in its factories:
The Works of men erupt along the countryside.

WAITING FOR THE BUS

She hung away her years, her eyes grew young,
    And filled the dress that filled the shop;
Her figure softened into summer, though wind stung
    And rain would never stop.

    A dreaming not worn out with knowing,
A moment's absence from the watch, the weather.
    I threw the paper down, that carried no such story,
But roared for what it could not have, perpetual health
              and liberty and glory.
    It whirled away, a lost bedraggled feather.

Then have we missed the bus? Or are we sure
             which way the wind is blowing?

AN EGYPTIAN IN BIRMINGHAM

Behind the black barrage the Northern phantoms gather:
Whole winters huddle, weeks of wet Walpurgis,
and hour by hour
The Dane's uneasy twilight smothers me, in
Clouds that weep a monstrous European misery —
And my stiff dread of living free and lonely, unconfined
and cold.

Although each drop of rain be sibilant, a sibyl, be
syllable of history,
Give me my Sun, shameless and gross and full of cruel humours.
Surely the world's burst conscience overhangs this island —
Shall I drown in the sorrows that flood in with the wind?

— Sorrows not my own, when I have more than many?
Starved of my shih-shah, tric-trac, and the click-clack
of consoling friends —
How we drowned our lusts in endless anecdote, sweetened
All small humiliations with our honeyed memories!
O Hassan, Ahmed, Ibrahim, our lives had grown to myths —
But now, what fun could even Goha find, in Birmingham?

And if, one dreary morning, I should stand and cry,
My tongue erect with God again, outside the cold clean
Civic Centre —
What drama follows, what vast emotions writhe across the
busy squares?
A sombre large policeman with a low-pitched voice,
A cautious muffled Justice, snuffling and indistinct.

At home the sea would smile and smile, while near the shore
The suave shark rolled, like some notorious pasha:
We flocked to the sea's edge like a monarch's welcome

Warmed our hearts with curses, our bellies with the meat
                    of argument,
Until they sank together, monstrous sun and monstrous fish.

Home is made of love and hate: the beggar's incantation
Clamoured about me where church bells now complain:
Tyranny ran us down in city streets, with klaxons sneering —
Yet Freedom lounged in every alley, no man too poor
To buy her hourly, for a broad story or a smaller coin.
The fat king himself, our daytime devil, we worshipped
                    in dreams, our hero by night —
In suffering we bought him, weight for weight — he was ours!
Crouched on the smarting sand, my ruined people wept and wailed
Till the great moon came out, royal in blood and gold,
And stared between our heads across a vast and jewelled sky,
Till the tears became laughing, our bruises voluptuous,
And giggling we counted our scars.

But here the crowds stride on like zombies: green and red
The dead lights guide my safe and sullen steps —
                    arms useless
At my sides, my tongue is frozen, its flowers all dead —
But wait, when I go home, you too, Birmingham, you
Shall be marvellous, your fame ripple through the bazaars
                    like a belly dancer —
A city of peril, like the shark, a city of witty Gohas,
Your streets astream with passions, big as buses,
Brown jinn shall squat upon your chimneys, ravage the
                    countryside —
Your chanting pigeons, at evening, be princesses and enchanted.

When I am home, and my bored days flame up in brilliant story.

THE BEACH AT ABOUSIR

Nature does justice here to man, whatever man may do
                            to man;
Though equally unplanned her actions. So the factions
Of the proud uprising wave submerge the crowded bands
Of sharp and silver sand. The nervous scrambling crab,
                          perpetual refugee,
Is stranded by war's tide, and on his wasted legs
Runs to recover what is ever being lost for ever.
                          Yet the sea-medusa,
Richer blue in that rich blue, lolls in a looser motion
Up and down, drowning and never drowned.

Against the dazzling silver, dull unreflecting rags;
Between the Sunday cars, those pointed brittle shapes,
                       like trees in winter —
Aged men and ancient children. Patient,
They watch their chance, to steal a towel or cushion,
Or else receive, from passionless bathers, some piastres.
                      Masters and peasants,
The banks of silver sand, the clutching hand —
                     for us between —
Too hard, too hard, to live between the black and white,
Under a wordless sun, too bright, where no committee
                    snips the Gordian knot.
But suddenly the knife is lifted. Under the waves
Of rippling stars, the sagging moon, a sole voice raves.

A DEMONSTRATION

Among the starting birds, the gentle hunters stroke their
                                       curving boats,
Between the darting fish. Along the moon-washed waters
                                     of this splintered lake,
Their beaks peer through the reeds, the thin poles hardly shake
                                     its green and living skin.
Here arid unpoetic Africa is suave. No human angers sway them,
As they hunt their birds and fishes. Silent, simple,
                                     so absorbed,
These figures, painted in with single strokes, a master's pen.

And then the cry is heard, that their oppression smells to heaven,
That those shall know of it, whose blunted nostrils breathe in
                                     Bourse and Palace.
The messenger is blood. And now some unknown native alien –
Far from the Athens that he never knew, the Bourse he never
                                     entered –
Drives the fishes into hiding, scares the birds away.
                                  Under the sun he smells to heaven.
The Bourse still chokes with old tobacco smoke, the Palace
                                     with its royal scents.

THE ACROPOLIS

We found no white and perfect temples —
      no burnished marbles
Under no bright sun, no brilliant sky.

Armed against the old concomitants,
      we found none —
Donkey's or driver's dung, fake findings,
The clever beverage, *bien glacé.*

Dark throttled winds shook here and there,
The air was grey with shattered columns,
      and shuddered.

Areopagus crouched below, that bleak rock
Cold and criminal, with its disappointed
      furious hole.

Before the caryatids' icy stare,
      the tourists scurried —
A long road ran them back to happier Athens
      and the heat.

DEATH IN THE SOUTH

Whatever snows embrace the soul, you'll have
                    your body lie
In this warm populous land: where its last sigh

Is lost in all the gabble of the frogs, and
                    that high
Sing-song of the tireless crickets. The long cry

Of love and living jars the plump and scented
                    sleeping sky
To starry splinters. Oh, remote from that dry

Silence of the stopped machines. And far from where
                    the nightingale will die,
Sole and eccentric, its histrionic death. You choose to lie

Where life will never let you rest. And if the choirs deny
Their voices, you'll have what the crickets and the frogs
                    supply.

THE LAUGHING HYENA, AFTER HOKUSAI

For him, it seems, everything was molten. Court-ladies flow
                    in gentle streams,
Or, gathering lotus, strain sideways from their curving boat,
A donkey prances, or a kite dances in the sky, or soars
                    like sacrificial smoke.
All is flux: waters fall and leap, and bridges leap and fall.
Even his Tortoise undulates, and his Spring Hat is lively
                    as a pool of fish.
All he ever saw was sea: a sea of marble splinters —
Long bright fingers claw across his pages, fjords and islands
                    and shattered trees —

And the Laughing Hyena, cavalier of evil, as volcanic
                    as the rest:
Elegant in a flowered gown, a face like a bomb-burst,
Featured with fangs and built about a rigid laugh,
Ever moving, like a pond's surface where a corpse has sunk.

Between the raised talons of the right hand rests an object —
At rest, like a pale island in a savage sea —
                    a child's head,
Immobile, authentic, torn and bloody —
The point of repose in the picture, the point of movement
                    in us.

Terrible enough, this demon. Yet it is present and perfect,
Firm as its horns, curling among its thick and handsome hair.
I find it an honest visitant, even consoling, after all
Those sententious phantoms, choked with rage and uncertainty
Who grimace from contemporary pages. It, at least,
Knows exactly why it laughs.

BREAD RATHER THAN BLOSSOMS
(Japan)

THE MONUMENTS OF HIROSHIMA

The roughly estimated ones, who do not sort well
    with our common phrases,
Who are by no means eating roots of dandelion,
    or pushing up the daisies.

The more or less anonymous, to whom no human idiom
    can apply,
Who neither passed away, or on,
    nor went before, nor vanished on a sigh.

Little of peace for them to rest in, less of them
    to rest in peace:
Dust to dust a swift transition, ashes to ash
    with awful ease.

Their only monument will be of others' casting —
A Tower of Peace, a Hall of Peace, a Bridge of Peace
    — who might have wished for something lasting,
Like a wooden box.

THE SHORT LIFE OF KAZUO YAMAMOTO

At the age of thirteen, you passed by the park
Of Nakanoshima, you paused by the Public Library
                    with its well-fed shelves.
The queue outside could have kept you for weeks,
Except that students shine their shoes themselves.

You swallowed the rat poison, all the easier
                    for having a healthy appetite,
And died with admirable definition. Your last words
Were even reported in the papers. 'I wanted to die
Because of a headache.' The policeman took it down,
                    adding that you were quite
Alone and had no personal belongings, other than a
            headache.

Elsewhere the great ones have their headaches, too,
As they grapple with those notable tongue-twisters
Such as Liberation and Oppression.
                    But they were not talking about you,
Kazuo, who found rat poison cheaper than aspirin.

THE RAG-PICKER'S FEAST

He must yield up his jovial beard,
The warm red robe and furry boots are taken back.
He walks away, with pay and frailer perquisites,
Toys bent or broken from the bottom of his sack —

To strip anew some long denuded neighbourhood;
So quick to know the worn from the worn-out
And what is trash from what has once been good.
The beard has left an itch, one more to scratch.

The children do not run to him nor run away;
Unnoticed now he goes, one other wind-swept rag
That preaches resurrection to the hopeless bins;
As nameless as the cats who share his bag.

A tinsel strand calls back his cryptic glory —
He wraps it in a paper, reads how foreign Christians cry
(Their shopping done) 'Put Christ back into Christmas.'
The rag-man hoists his sack, 'Make Christmas longer,'
            with a sigh.

A KYOTO GARDEN

(for Bunshō Jugaku)

Here you could pass your holidays,
        trace and retrace the turning ways,
a hundred yards of stepping stones, you feel
        yourself a traveller; alone

you skirt a range of moss, you cross
        and cross again what seem new Rubicons,
a *tan* of land will make ten prefectures,
        a tideless pond a great pacific sea;

each vista, you remark, seems the intended prize —
        like Fuji through a spider's web or else
between a cooper's straining thighs —
        the eyes need never be averted, nor the nose;

across a two-foot fingered canyon, an Amazon of dew,
        a few dwarf maples
lose you in a forest, then you gain a mole-hill's
        panoramic view,

and company enough, a large anthology —
        the golden crow, the myriad leaves,
the seven autumn flowers, the seven herbs of spring,
        the moon sends down a rice-cake and a cassia-tree

till under a sliding foot a pebble shrieks:
        you hesitate —
what feeds this corpulent moss, whose emptied blood,
        what demon mouths await? —

but then you notice that the pines wear crutches —
        typhoons show no respect for art or craft;
you sigh with happiness, the garden comes alive:
        like us, these princelings feel the draught.

MAD POET

He dances on his naked native toe,
And stars and blots and jottings sport about his head,
Read or unread, his works lie in a silken pile,
Beneath the unpacific sky he dances, while
The autumn pine drops leaves of thought about his head.

One agile line creates him in his twisted robe,
From toe to glorious grin and balding top —
Apply for special status, in return for quip and quirk?
Straightened shall be your crooked line, and stopped
                     your hop!
Pick up your careless leaves and sort your thoughts,
Replace the stars in heaven, modify that smirk!

              It is alleged
An empty saké bottle in your company was seen.
No more than drunk you are, on Old Japan —
So far as we can tell, undemocratic Poet San.

THE PIED PIPER OF AKASHI :

A Japanese Tale

Despite the striking rows on rows of little stones,
    and large statistics,
Despite the vivid rags and ill-consorting bones —
    a fairy tale alone can make it real and true.

At ten in the morning the black planes flew
    across to bomb the factory
That made black planes. A happy harmless time of day
For children and the aged, both at their various play.

The young ones and old ones scurried to the park,
    the pretty refuge of the useless and the refuse
Of the race. Away from the dark planes in the sky,
    the dark planes on the ground.

But in the morning brightness, the dazed planes found
A human target, by a human error, and let their sleeping
    brothers lie.
They taught the pines a lesson, the grass repented its
    aggression. While nearby
The factory shuddered slightly at the sight.

That night the workers, back from perilous bench or office,
Found their home-town queerly run to middle age —
    no imps of sons, no docile daughters,
And hardly any ancients, whether cracked or sage.

Time, though, and our native riches have once again refuted
    the frozen spell of elves
And witches. New old were soon recruited,
    from ourselves.

The young sprang up afresh, careless of wrongs and rights,
    to shame the frailer rice
And harass our economy. They filled the ownerless kimonos,
    and flew their dusty brothers' kites.

The park is full of bold and bandy babies, and a glory
Of chrysanthemums and paper bags. The nearby factory is full
Of busy adults, glittering planes, and foreign capital —
    a kindly fairy ends our little story.

BLUE UMBRELLAS

'The thing that makes a blue umbrella with its tail —
How do you call it?' you ask. Poorly and pale
Comes my answer. For all I can call it is peacock.

Now that you go to school, you will learn how we
        call all sorts of things;
How we mar great works by our mean recital.
You will learn, for instance, that Head Monster
        is not the gentleman's accepted title;
The blue-tailed eccentrics will be merely peacocks;
        the dead bird will no longer doze
Off till tomorrow's lark, for the letter has killed him.
The dictionary is opening, the gay umbrellas close.

        Oh our mistaken teachers! —
It was not a proper respect for words that we need,
But a decent regard for things, those older creatures
        and more real.
Later you may even resort to writing verse
To prove the dishonesty of names and their black greed —
To confess your ignorance, to expiate your crime,
        seeking a spell to lift a curse.
Or you may, more commodiously, spy on your children,
        busy discoverers,
Without the dubious benefit of rhyme.

NATURE POETRY

I was regarding the famous trees, locked in the case
Of a glassy sky, as dignified as some dead face,
As dead as well.
              Until my daughter scampered up, gabbling
Of the famous monkeys in the zoo. And the trees were
                      suddenly scrabbling
In the air, they glowed, they shook with communal rage.
For the trees were bereaved of monkeys. And in the zoo
The bitter monkeys shook the dead iron of their cage.

HAPPY NEW YEAR

An avalanche of cards, a thousand calligraphic miles,
        assure a bright New Year.
And yet and yet, I met a banker weeping through his smiles,
        upon that hectic morn.

Omedetō, he told me while the saké bubbled on his lips.
His frock-coat trembled in its new and yearly bliss.
'A hard year for Japan,' he said, and gurgled out a sigh.
'A hard grim year.' A saké-smelling tear suffused his
        reddened eye.

He clapped me by the hand, he led me to his bright new
        house.
He showed his ancient incense burners, precious treasures,
        cold and void.
His family too he showed, drawn up in columns, and his
        fluttering spouse.
We bowed and wept together over the grim new year.

I walked away, my head was full of yen,
        of falling yen.
I saw the others with their empty pockets,
Merry on the old year's dregs, their mouths distilled
        a warm amen!

The poor are always with us. Only they
        can find a value in the new.
They are the masters of their fourpenny kites
That soar in the open market of the sky.
Whatever wrongs await, they still preserve some rites.

THE FIGHT AGAINST ILLITERACY

The wreckage of reviews, the offal of off-prints,
                    litter my desk.
In the paddy-field an ancient woman spoons to each
                    young plant its ration
Of hot harsh food. So small, so single, so delicate,
                    her bowels melt with compassion.

The arrogant cobwebs shout out for humility,
The grave intellectuals are doing their strip-tease —
I am told I resemble what the rice is reared on —
Despair — the well-fed writers cry — Down, down on
                    your knees —

Down on her knees the ancient woman soothes her rice.
I shall teach her to read what the gentlemen write.
She will scream and run off, trampling the rice to jelly.
                    And the spiders shall cease to spin,
As the pain in the neck descends to the belly,
                    where lessons begin.

PUBLIC ADDRESS SYSTEM

Shaken with smoke, high over the shunting, a voice
                                    is chanting,
That this is the city, the city, o thank you
Honourable passengers, for your precious patronage,
Forgive our facilities, crowded and comfortless,
And this is the city, the city, the city.

And the sober burst out and the drunk stumble in,
Umbrellas and brief-cases, students and labourers,
Gay lads from sad villages, sad girls from gay quarters,
All honourable, honourable, overlords and underlings,
We come and we go, and up in the girders the voice
                                    ever chanting,
O honourable passengers, with honourable tickets,
O thank you, o honourable whistles and honourable
                                    slammings —
And this is the city, the city, the city.

Over bare rails, when the last train has started,
                                    another voice wails,
That those were real people, real people, real people,
Sold for the cost of a cocktail party, sick for the
                                    price of a square meal, maybe —
But welcome o passengers and farewell o passengers,
For honourable hearts can abstain from remarking
What honourable eyes may happen to see —
                                    for this is the city, the city, the city. . .

THE OLD MAN COMES TO HIS SENSES

Potter's field; where everything is used
And broken;
       in love and strife
The old and new are lost; the ants run
Over all; where art dies back to life.

Mount Hiei scowls; scarred with the sherds
Of history and burnt-out creeds;
       where the bellicose monks
Jostle the mild merchants of *tanka;* and in
The sacred wood, ghostly profundities wail
Among the scaly trunks.
       Where those who have pierced the veil
Are mumbling their thin curds;
The soulful skeletons bat their sleeves.

Drop me in potter's field; where whatever is
       done to me
Is wholly explicable and no more than I deserve —
Among these merry bones; bottles that were drunk
With joy; cups that have overflowed; vases
That held a year of flowers —
       smelling the nostrils of the dog,
Under the flat feet of the poor, knowing the nerve
Of the grasshopper, and the spring of the frog;
       and ants running over all.

33

IN THE HANKYU ELECTRIC

Musing on the hour of commuting, in the Hankyu Electric,
        when the hectic rice-winners,
Drowsing on the crowded benches, drop their work-day faces
— The tight lips droop, the thin cheeks fall away,
        in sleep's decay —
You would not think they were natural at all.

Musing on the sayings of reviewers, in the Hankyu Electric,
        'Mr. Enright's language is eclectic',
'His artistry is patent' (or, his flippancy is blatant),
'His themes are generally exotic' (he cannot manage the demotic) —
You would not think he was natural at all.

Musing on the long-necked bamboos, along the Hankyu Electric,
        as the bright breeze shakes them,
They squeak and crake and clutter, like apoplectic birds,
        they utter cutting words —
You would not think they were natural at all.

SOME MEN ARE BROTHERS

(South-East Asia, Berlin, Japan)

THE POOR WAKE UP QUICKLY

Surprised at night,
The trishaw driver
Slithers from the carriage,
Hurls himself upon the saddle.

With what violence he peddles
Slapbang into the swarming night,
Neon skidding off his cheekbones!
Madly he makes away
In the wrong direction.
I tap his shoulder nervously.
Madly he turns about
Between the taxis and the trams,
Makes away electric-eyed
In another wrong direction.

How do I star in that opium dream?
A hulking red-faced ruffian
Who beats him on his bony back,
Cursing in the tongue of demons.
But when we're there
He grumbles mildly over his wage,
Like a sober man,
A man who has had no recent visions.
The poor wake up quickly.

A POLISHED PERFORMANCE

Citizens of the polished capital
   Sigh for the towns up country,
And their innocent simplicity.

People in the towns up country
   Applaud the unpolished innocence
Of the distant villages.

Dwellers in the distant villages
   Speak of a simple unspoilt girl,
Living alone, deep in the bush.

Deep in the bush we found her,
   Large and innocent of eye,
Among gentle gibbons and mountain ferns.

Perfect for the part, perfect,
   Except for the dropsy
Which comes from polished rice.

In the capital our film is much admired,
   Its gentle gibbons and mountain ferns,
Unspoilt, unpolished, large and innocent of eye.

This is how it was. Just one minute particular.
Particular, though minute. With no additions

(Titles are easy), no decorations (two sides
To every medal), no deep deductions (words drawn
            from words) —

No description of the hovel where they fetched him from;
No description of the hovel where they took him to

(I would not distract you with such word-paintings,
You should not think my theme the building-styles of Angst).

— As for his history: this is not a novel
(If only it were novel!) For his occupation —

I'm no UNESCO Fellow, this no report on peasant skills
(Anyone can die, and he was helped to).

Simply, he was human, did no harm, and suffered for it.
His name? — We might be tempted by its liquid vowels,
            the richness of its rhythms —

I've said too much already.
            Writers of epitaphs, in your conceit, remember:
There may be relatives still living.

SPOTTED DEER

The white-spotted deer had lots of everything;
But the black-spotted deer had only a little.

So the white-spots sent the black-spots stacks of food,
For which the black-spots were properly grateful.

The white-spots also sent the black-spots knives and forks
To eat the food with, and the black-spots said, 'Thank you'.

Later the white-spots presented pleasant sets of dishes
For the black-spots to eat their pleasant food off.

These were followed by artistic napkins, all embroidered
'To the Black-spots: From their friends the White-spots'.

A professor white-spot came to teach the black-spots
How to sit at a table and eat their nice food nicely.

Of course the black-spots listened with respect,
For White-spot Edible Aid was full of vitamins and savour.

Then the white-spots equipped the black-spots with guided
                                    antlers,
To cope with the red-spots whom the smell of food had
                                    attracted.

And the black-spots put on the antlers back to front,
Remarking uneasily that 'Under the circumstances' etc.

A doctor white-spot arrived to instruct the black-spots
In the construction of latrines to cope with the increased etc.

Whereupon the black-spots invoked an ancient tradition
Forbidding the digging of holes in the breast of Mother Earth.

A white-spot cultural envoy was gored by black-spot students,
And the red-spots were attracted by the smell of foodlessness.

This coolness continued till low-level changes took place
In both governments and some new traditions were uncovered.

AM STEINPLATZ

Benches round a square of grass.
You enter by the stone that asks,
    'Remember those whom Hitlerism killed'.
'Remember those whom Stalinism killed',
Requests the stone by which you leave.

This day, as every other day,
I shuffle through the little park,
    from stone to stone,
From conscience-cancelling stone to stone,
Peering at the fading ribbons on the faded wreaths.

At least the benches bear their load,
Of people reading papers, eating ices,
Watching aeroplanes and flowers,
Sleeping, smoking, counting, cuddling.
        Everything but heed those stony words.
They have forgotten. As they must.
Remember those who live. Yes, they are right.
        They must.

A dog jumps on the bench beside me.
Nice doggie: never killed a single Jew, or Gentile.
Then it jumps on me. Its paws are muddy, muzzle wet.
Gently I push it off. It likes this game of war.

At last a neat stout lady on a nearby bench
Calls tenderly, 'Komm, Liebchen, komm!
Der Herr' — this public-park-frau barks —
        'does not like dogs!'

Shocked papers rustle to the ground;
Ices drip away forgotten; sleepers wake;
The lovers mobilise their distant eyes.
        The air strikes cold.
There's no room for a third stone here.
        I leave.

NO OFFENCE

In no country
Are the disposal services more efficient.

Standardised dustbins
Fit precisely into the mouth of a large cylinder
Slung on a six-wheeled chassis.
Even the dustbin lid is raised mechanically
At the very last moment.
You could dispose of a corpse like this
Without giving the least offence.

In no country
Are the public lavatories more immaculately kept.
As neat as new pins, smelling of pine forests,
With a roar like distant Wagner
Your sins are washed away.

In no country
Do the ambulances arrive more promptly.
You are lying on the stretcher
Before the police, the driver, the bystanders and the
                                        neighbouring shopkeepers
Have finished lecturing you.

In no country
Are the burial facilities more foolproof.
A few pfennigs a week, according to age,
Will procure you a very decent funeral.
You merely sign on the dotted line
And keep your payments regular.

In no country
Are the disposal services more efficient
– I reflect –
As I am sorted out, dressed down, lined up,

Shepherded through the door,
Marshalled across the smooth-faced asphalt,
And fed into the mouth of a large cylinder
Labelled 'Lufthansa'.

KYOTO IN AUTUMN

Precarious hour. Moment of charity and the
        less usual love.

Mild evening. Even taxis now fall mild.
Grey heart, grey city, grey and dusty dove.

Retiring day peers back through paper windows;
        here and there a child
Digs long-lost treasure from between her feet.

Where yesterday the sun's staff beat,
        where winter's claws tomorrow sink,
The silent ragman picks his comfort now.

The straitened road holds early drunkards
        like a stronger vow;
The season's tang renews the burning tongue.

Poetic weather, nowhere goes unsung,
However short the song. A pipe's smoke prints
Its verses on the hand-made paper of that sky;

And under lanterns leaping like struck flints,
        a potter's novice squats
And finds his colours in the turning air.

A pallid grace invests the gliding cars.
The Kamo keeps its decent way, not opulent nor bare.
The last light waves a fading hand. Now fiercer seasons
        start like neon in the little bars.

CHANGING THE SUBJECT

I had suggested, in exasperation, that he find
    something other to write about
Than the moon, and flowers, and birds, and temples,
    and the bare hills of the once holy city —

People, I proposed, who bravely push their way
    through the leprous lakes of mud.
It was the wet season, rain upon spittle and urine,
    and I had been bravely pushing my way.

It happened my hard words chimed with a new slogan,
    a good idea, since ruined —
'Humanism'. So I helped on a fashion, another like
    mambo, French chanson, and learning Russian.

Now he comes back, my poet, in a different guise:
    the singer of those who sleep in the subway.
'Welcome you are,' his vagrants declaim to each other,
    'a comrade of the common fate.'

'Are they miners from Kyushu?' he asks, these 'hobos
    all in rags.' And adds that
'Broken bamboo baskets, their constant companions, watch
    loyally over their sleeping masters.'

Thus my friend. He asks me if he has passed the test,
    is he truly humanistic,
Will I write another article, about his change of heart?
    I try to think of the subway sleepers.

Who are indescribable. Have no wives or daughters to sell.
  Not the grain of faith that makes a beggar.
Have no words. No thing to express. No 'comrade'.
  Nothing so gratifying as a 'common fate'.

Their broken bamboo baskets are loyal because no one
  would wish to seduce them.
Their ochre skin still burns in its black nest, though a
  hundred changed poets decide to sing them.

'Are they miners from Kyushu?' Neither he nor I will
  ever dare to ask them.
For we know they are not really human, are as apt themes
  for verse as the moon and the bare hills.

THE NOODLE-VENDOR'S FLUTE

In a real city, from a real house,
At midnight by the ticking clocks,
In winter by the crackling roads:
Hearing the noodle-vendor's flute,
Two single fragile falling notes . . .
But what can this small sing-song say,
Under the noise of war?
The flute itself a counterfeit
(Siberian wind can freeze the lips),
Merely a rubber bulb and metal horn
(Hard to ride a cycle, watch for manholes
And late drunks, and play a flute together).
Just squeeze between gloved fingers,
And the note of mild hope sounds:
Release, the indrawn sigh of mild despair . . .
A poignant signal, like the cooee
Of some diffident soul locked out,
Less than appropriate to cooling macaroni.
Two wooden boxes slung across the wheel,
A rider in his middle age, trundling
This gross contraption on a dismal road,
Red eyes and nose and breathless rubber horn.
Yet still the pathos of that double tune
Defies its provenance, and can warm
The bitter night.
Sleepless, we turn and sleep.
Or sickness dwindles to some local limb.
Bought love for one long moment gives itself.
Or there a witch assures a frightened child
She bears no personal grudge.
And I, like other listeners,

See my stupid sadness as a common thing.
And being common,
Therefore something rare indeed.
The puffing vendor, surer than a trumpet,
Tell us we are not alone.
Each night that same frail midnight tune
Squeezed from a bogus flute,
Under the noise of war, after war's noise,
It mourns the fallen, every night,
It celebrates survival —
In real cities, real houses, real time.

BUSYBODY UNDER A CHERRY TREE

The pasteboard houses and the plywood schools
Are shaken with their monstrous living load,
Though everywhere blind highways and dark pools
Wait to divert the careless or the indisposed.

Here in a patch of sick maltreated earth,
Much written of but not too proud for this
The cherry comes to its immaculate birth.

This tree reminds the busybody
That falling hopes are not so absolute as falling
                                        hairs,
That beauty needs and often gets no civic welcome,
That the half-educated still can love, and theirs
May be the whole which we shall never dare,

And that the cherry's body all year round is busy
Against one week of showered gifts without advice,
For it is silent, for its deeds suffice.

DISPLACED PERSON LOOKS AT A CAGE-BIRD

Every single day, going to where I stay
    (how long?), I pass the canary
In the window. Big bird, all pranked out,
Looming and booming in the window's blank.

Closing a pawky eye, tapping its hairy chest,
    flexing a brawny wing.
Every single day, coming from where I stay
(How long?), I pass this beastly thing.

How I wish it were dead!
    — Florid, complacent, rent-free and over-fed,
Feather-bedded, pensioned, free from wear and tear,
Earth has not anything to show less fair.

I do wish it were dead!
    Then I'd write a better poetry,
On that poor wee bird, its feet in the air,
An innocent victim of something. Just like me.

A PLEASANT WALK

This sudden wintry country sun
Reminds me of a walk I used to take:
Though that was far away, and in Japan
A road's the only thing they cannot make.

This was an altogether special case,
A noble promenade called Midōsuji:
Contained by banks and trees, it was a place
As sacrosanct though better kept than Fuji.

Pavements ever shining, an air that never stank,
I loitered past the Mercantile, Dai-Ichi Ginkō,
Sanwa, Chase National and Netherlands Handelsbank,
Under the spreading silver of the princely gingkō.

That was a healthy and a pleasing walk:
No beggar cursed the view and no one ever spat
Before the Nippon Kangyō or National City of New York.
High commerce civilises, there is no doubt of that.

Preserve me from the brutal village sunk in slush;
Allow me Midōsuji, paved in gold from every nation,
Where no dishonoured kitten breaks the busy hush
Of the Hongkong and Shanghai Banking Corporation.

This apparition of a wintry country sun
Reminds me of the walk that now I lack —
Near by the Yodo River, as quiet as any nun,
Where grill and guichet hold the violent city back.

SAYING NO

After so many (in so many places) words,
It came to this one, No.
Epochs of parakeets, of peacocks, of paradisiac birds —
Then one bald owl croaked, No.

And now (in this one place, one time) to celebrate,
One sound will serve.
After the love-laced talk of art, philosophy and fate —
Just, No.

Some virtue here, in this speech-stupefied inane,
To keep it short.
However cumbrous, puffed and stretched the pain —
To say no more than, No.

Virtue (or only decency) it would have been,
But — no.
I dress that death's-head, all too plain, too clean,
With lots of pretty lengths of saying,

No.

THE QUAGGA

By mid-century there were two quaggas left,
And one of the two was male.
The cares of office weighed heavily on him.
When you are the only male of a species,
It is not easy to lead a normal sort of life.

The goats nibbled and belched in casual content;
They charged and skidded up and down their concrete
                                mountain.
One might cut his throat on broken glass,
Another stray too near the tigers.
But they were zealous husbands; and the enclosure
                                was always full,
Its rank air throbbing with ingenuous voices.

The quagga, however, was a man of destiny.
His wife, whom he had met rather late in her life,
Preferred to sleep, or complain of the food and
                                the weather.
For their little garden was less than paradisiac,
With its artificial sun that either scorched or left
                                you cold,
And savants with cameras eternally hanging around,
To perpetuate the only male quagga in the world.

Perhaps that was why he failed to do it himself.
It is all very well for goats and monkeys —
But the last male of a species is subject to peculiar
                                pressures.
If ancient Satan had come slithering in, perhaps . . .
But instead the savants, with cameras and notebooks,
Writing sad stories of the decadence of quaggas.

And then one sultry afternoon he started raising Cain.
This angry young quagga kicked the bars and broke a
                              camera;
He even tried to bite his astonished keeper.
He protested loud and clear against this and that,
Till the other animals became quite embarrassed
For he seemed to be calling them names.

Then he noticed his wife, awake with the noise,
And a curious feeling quivered round his belly.
He was Adam: there was Eve.
Galloping over to her, his head flung back,
He stumbled, and broke a leg, and had to be shot.

ADDICTIONS

(Japan, South-East Asia, Berlin)

IN MEMORIAM

How clever they are, the Japanese, how clever!
The great department store, Takashimaya, on the
Ginza, near Maruzen Bookshop and British Council —
A sky-scraper swaying with every earth-tremor,
Bowing and scraping, but never falling (how clever!).
On the roof-garden of tall Takashimaya lives an
Elephant. How did he get there, that clever Japanese
Elephant? By lift? By helicopter? (How clever,
Either way.) And this young man who went there to teach
(Uncertificated, but they took him) in Tokyo,
This Englishman with a fine beard and a large and
(It seemed) a healthy body.

                     And he married an orphan,
A Japanese orphan (illegitimate child of
A geisha — Japanese for 'a clever person' — and a
Number of customers), who spoke no English and
He spoke no Japanese. (But how clever they were!)
For a year they were married. She said, half in Japanese,
Half in English, wholly in truth: 'This is the first time
I have known happiness.' (The Japanese are a
Clever people, clever but sad.) 'They call it a
Lottery,' he wrote to me, 'I have made a lucky dip.'
(She was a Japanese orphan, brought up in a convent.)
At the end of that year he started to die.
They flew him to New York, for 2-million volt treatment
('Once a day,' he wrote, 'Enough to make you sick!')
And a number of operations. 'They say there's a
90% chance of a cure,' he wrote, 'Reversing
The odds, I suspect.' Flying back to his orphan,
He was removed from the plane at Honolulu and
Spent four days in a slummy hotel with no money or
Clothes. His passport was not in order. (Dying men
Are not always clever enough in thinking ahead.)

They operated again in Tokyo and again,
He was half a man, then no man, but the cancer
Throve on it. 'All I can say is,' he wrote in November,
'Takashimaya will damned well have to find
Another Father Christmas this year, that's all.'
(It was. He died a week later. I was still puzzling
How to reply.)

                      He would have died anywhere.
And he lived his last year in Japan, loved by a
Japanese orphan, teaching her the rudiments of
Happiness, and (without certificate) teaching
Japanese students. In the dungeons of learning, the
Concentration campuses, crammed with ragged uniforms
And consumptive faces, in a land where the literacy
Rate is over 100%, and the magazines
Read each other in the crowded subways. And
He was there (clever of them!), he was there teaching.
Then she went back to her convent, the Japanese
Widow, having known a year's happiness with a
Large blue-eyed red-bearded foreign devil, that's all.
There is a lot of cleverness in the world, but still
Not enough.

REFLECTIONS ON FOREIGN LITERATURE

The stories which my friends compose are very sad.
They border on the morbid (which, in the literatures
Of foreign languages, we may licitly enjoy, for they
    cannot really
Corrupt, any more than we can be expected to discriminate).

(Sometimes I ask myself: Do I live in foreign countries
Because they cannot corrupt me, because I cannot be
Expected to make the unending effort of discrimination?
The exotic: a rest from meaning.)

('The officer shall engage in no activities whatsoever
Of a political nature,' says my contract, 'in the area where
    he serves.'
And all activity, it seems, is political.)

Anyway, the stories of my friends are very sad.
I am afraid they are largely true, too, discounting the
    grace-notes of my elegant friends.
At the heart of the ideogram is a suffering man or woman.

I remember my friend's friend, a barmaid in Shinjuku,
    at a literary pub —
Neither snowy-skinned nor sloe-eyed (though far from slow-
    witted),
Neither forward nor backward, of whom my friend
(A former P.E.N. delegate) said in a whisper:
'Her life-story would make a book. I shall tell you one day . . . '
The day never came. But I can imagine the story.

My friend's friend also made special ties out of leather;
My friend gave me one, as a parting gift, a special memory
    of his country.

It has an elegant look; but when I wear it, it chafes my skin;
Whispering that nothing is exotic, if you understand,
    if you stick your neck out for an hour or two;
That only the very worst literature is foreign;
That practically no life at all is.

CONFESSIONS OF AN ENGLISH OPIUM SMOKER

In some sobriety
I offer to recall those images:
Damsel, dome and dulcimer,
Portentous pageants, alien altars,
Foul unimaginable imagined monster,
Façades of fanfares, Lord's Prayer
Tattooed backwards on a Manchu fingernail,
Enigma, or a dread too well aware,
Swirling curtains, almond eyes or smell?

And I regain these images:
Rocked by the modern traffic of the town,
A grubby, badly lighted, stuffy shack —
A hollow in some nobody's family tree,
The undistinguished womb of anybody's
Average mother. And then me,
In all sobriety, slight pain in neck and back,
Expecting that and then a little more,
Right down to bed-rock.
This was no coloured twopenny,
Just a common people's penny sheet —

To read with cool avidity.
(What would you do with dulcimers,
And damsels, and such embarrassments?
Imagined beasts more foul than real monsters?
No man at peace makes poetry.)
Thus I recall, despite myself, the images
That merely were. I offer my sedate respects
To those so sober entertainments,
Suited to our day and ages.

THE BURNING OF THE PIPES

Bangkok, 1 July, 1959

Who would imagine they were government property? —
Wooden cylinders with collars of silver, coming
From China, brown and shiny with sweat and age.
Inside them were banks of dreams, shiny with
Newness, though doubtless of time-honoured stock.
They were easy to draw on: you pursed your lips
As if to suckle and sucked your breath as if to
Sigh: two skills which most of us have mastered.

The dreams themselves weren't government property.
Rather, the religion of the people. While the state
Took its tithes and the compliance of sleepers.
Now a strong government dispenses with compliance,
A government with rich friends has no need of tithes.

What acrid jinn was it that entered their flesh?
For some, a magic saucer, over green enamelled
Parks and lofty flat-faced city offices, to
Some new Tamerlane in his ticker-tape triumph —
Romantics! They had been reading books.
Others found the one dream left them: dreamless sleep.

As for us, perhaps we had eaten too much to dream,
To need to dream, I mean, or have to sleep.
For us, a moment of thinking our thoughts were viable,
And hope not a hopeless pipe-dream; for us
The gift of forgiveness for the hole in the road,
The dog we ran over on our way to bed.
Wasn't that something? The Chinese invented so much.

64

A surprise to find they were government property
— Sweat-brown bamboo with dull silver inlay —
As they blaze in thousands on a government bonfire,
In the government park, by government order!
The rice crop is expected to show an increase,
More volunteers for the army, and navy, and
Government service, and a decrease in petty crime.

Not the first time that fire destroys a dream.
Coca-cola sellers slither through the crowd; bats
Agitate among the rain-trees; flash-bulbs pop.
A holocaust of wooden legs — a miracle constated!
Rubbing his hands, the Marshal steps back from
The smoke, lost in a dream of strong government.
Sad, but they couldn't be beaten into TV sets;
As tourist souvenirs no self-respecting state
Could sponsor them, even at thirty dollars each.

MAKING LOVE

Making love —
Love was what they'd made.
In rooms here and there,
In this town and that.
Something they had made —
Children to a childless pair.

Meeting now to unmake love,
To send this invitee
Who'd overstepped the bounds
Back where he belonged
(Though where did he belong?),
Easy come, they said, he'd easy go.

But love was what they'd made;
Acts turned to things.
These children of a childless pair
Had quickly put on weight,
And now stood round:
'Easier to make us than unmake.'

Such towering children they had made,
Not to be mislaid in hotel corridors,
Or shaken off in trains, or sleep.
And thus walled in,
What move could two small mortals make? —
They made love.

APOCALYPSE

'After the New Apocalypse, very few members were still
in possession of their instruments. Hardly a musician
could call a decent suit his own. Yet, by the early
summer of 1945, strains of sweet music floated on the
air again. While the town still reeked of smoke, charred
buildings and the stench of corpses, the Philharmonic
Orchestra bestowed the everlasting and imperishable joy
which music never fails to give.'

> (from *The Muses on the Banks of the Spree*,
> a Berlin tourist brochure.)

It soothes the savage doubts.
One Bach outweighs ten Belsens. If 200,000 people
Were remaindered at Hiroshima, the sales of So-and-So's
New novel reached a higher figure in as short a time.
So, imperishable paintings reappeared:
Texts were reprinted:
Public buildings reconstructed:
Human beings reproduced.

After the Newer Apocalypse, very few members
Were still in possession of their instruments
(Very few were still in possession of their members),
And their suits were chiefly indecent.
Yet, while the town still reeked of smoke etc.,
The Philharmonic Trio bestowed, etc.

A civilization vindicated,
A race with three legs still to stand on!
True, the violin was shortly silenced by leukaemia,
And the pianoforte crumbled softly into dust.
But the flute was left. And one is enough.
All, in a sense, goes on. All is in order.

And the ten-tongued mammoth larks,
The forty-foot crickets and the elephantine frogs
Decided that the little chap was harmless,
At least he made no noise, on the banks of whatever river
    it used to be.

One day, a reed-warbler stepped on him by accident.
However, all, in a sense, goes on. Still the everlasting
    and imperishable joy
Which music never fails to give is being given.

THE HARD CORE

You can find them anywhere.
In better managed states, you'll have to look:
They're there, unadvertised behind the hoardings,
In casual self-concealing tenements,
Asleep by public fountains.
In badly managed states, they walk the streets
Free citizens, free to beg.
      One is a junkie. Another armless.
One is spoiled by rheumatism (from working
Long hours on bridges or public fountains).
Some were born too weak to keep their strength up.
The commoner suffer merely from consumption,
And dysentery, and child-bearing, and anaemia.
Nothing, it seems, can dissolve this hard core
Of disorder and disease.
      The anarchist moves among them delicately
(Despite his age), with cast-off bread and
Clothing, small change and opium dottles,
Little gifts for his admirers
(As they would be, if they knew, if they'd had
The chance to know). They prove his point,
Without once opening their surly mouths.
They are the only people who count.
      He counts them.
Sometimes wondering, as he washes his hands
At a public fountain: Is he sorry?
Is he an anarchist because he is sorry?
Is he sorry because he's an anarchist?
Grateful, at last, when one of them spits
In his face. Breaking a law.

BARODA

The shy were not too shy;
The nationalistic not too nationalistic;
The Good-Old-Timers not incredible;
The poor were not too poor,
Or not too obvious.

A place where one might leave the heart
Ajar for some small emotion
Suited to the sarees and the gardens.
The gardens were soft and silky;
The sarees were gardens.

A betel chip built palaces in the mouth;
The Coffee Board's coffee (threepence a cup)
Was frankly enjoyable. As we left,
A small round cloud rolled over in the sky,
Enough to make a very decent tear.

BRUSH-FIRE

In a city of small pleasures,
    small spoils, small powers,
The wooden shacks are largely burning.
Bodies of small people lie along the shabby streets,
An old palace is smouldering.
Pushing bicycles piled with small bundles,
Families stream away, from north to south,
From south to north.

Who are these who are fighting those,
Fellow countrymen if not fellow men?
Some follow Prince X, some General Y.
Does Prince X lead the nobility, then,
And General Y the military?
Prince X is not particularly noble,
General Y is not so very military.
Some follow the Prince, for name's sake,
Or family's, or because he is there.
Some follow the General, for last month's pay,
Or family's sake, or because he walks in front.

Princes and generals have moderate ambitions.
An air-conditioned palace, a smarter G.H.Q.,
An Armstrong-Siddeley, another little wife.
The families, driven by some curious small ambition.
Stream away, from east to west, from west to east.
It is in their blood, to stream.
They know what is happening. None of them asks why —
They see that foreign tanks are running off
    with native drivers,
Foreign howitzers are manning native gunners —
As they pass by burning houses, on their way
    to burning houses.
Among such small people, the foreign shells
Make ridiculously big noises.

71

PARLIAMENT OF CATS

The cats caught a Yellow-vented Bulbul.
Snatched from them, for three days it uttered
Its gentle gospel, enthroned above their heads.
Became loved and respected of all the cats.
Then succumbed to internal injuries.
The cats regretted it all profoundly,
They would never forget the wrong they had done.

Later the cats caught a Daurian Starling.
And ate it. For a Daurian Starling is not
A Yellow-vented Bulbul. (Genuflection.)
Its colouring is altogether different.
It walks in a different, quite unnatural fashion.
The case is not the same at all as that of
The Yellow-vented Bulbul. (Genuflection.)

The kittens caught a Yellow-vented Bulbul.
And ate it. What difference, they ask, between
A Yellow-vented Bulbul and that known criminal
The Daurian Starling? Both move through the air
In a quite unnatural fashion. This is not
The Yellow-vented Bulbul of our parents' day,
Who was a Saint of course! (Genuflection.)

I WAS A GULLI-GULLI MAN'S CHICKEN

Come to terms with one's environment, you say?
Grass, grit and weather should be my environment:
I find myself a card, any card, in any pack of cards.

My master cannot do more than he can do.
(The greatest of beings suffers his own limitations.)
My master has almost come to terms with his environment.

Which means: Be startling but not shocking.
Be funny but clean. Be efficient but seem kindly.
He walks a tightrope. The tightrope is me.

Passed under summer frocks, I fight with elastic;
Planted in large bosoms, I beat my head on brassieres;
Marooned on barren waists, I skate on whalebone.

Do you know what human flesh smells like, as the
Whole of one's environment? The stuffiness of cotton,
The uncertainty of silk, the treachery of nylon?

Do you know that on the first-class deck, P & O,
My anus is lightly sewn up? The greatest of beings
Must please most of the people most of the time.

My master is all for cleanliness. How much
Cleanliness can a small animal like me endure?
How much being lost, do you think? How much handling?

They have invented toys which look like us.
It's little wonder that we living creatures
Should be held as toys. But cheaper, cheaper.

So I have come to terms with my environment.
Which is: hands that grasp me like a wheel or lever,
And an early (but at least organic) disappearance.

THE FAIRIES

Hard up at the time, the fairies gave me
    what they could: the gift
Of laying the right hand on the wrong door-knob.

Not the wits to profit from it —
    to hold the other hand palm upwards
Or open shop as a notable hot-headed reformer.

Just the gift itself, a robot's senseless gesture,
    which even bashfulness
(I was brought up humble) could not circumvent.

As I muse on the goodliness of my hosts,
    the capital food and wine and
The right-minded discourse, that hand goes out

And takes hold of the knob and turns it gently
    and the closet door swings eagerly open
And out falls a skeleton with a frightful crash.

Not that skeletons shock me. I possess no closets,
    but my suitcases are crammed with them.
All praise, I say, to him who doesn't run a boneyard.

But householders frown on my little gift,
    they impute an intention (politics,
I think they call it) far beyond my modest capacity.

'If your hand offends you, pluck it off' —
    so says my friend who is anxious for me
— 'You are only opening the door to the Enemy.'

There was a saying once: No one is perfect.
    But it seems we are, now,
We simply have to be. Goddam those seedy fairies

74

DREAMING IN THE SHANGHAI RESTAURANT

I would like to be that elderly Chinese gentleman.
He wears a gold watch with a gold bracelet,
But a shirt without sleeves or tie.
He has good luck moles on his face, but is not
    disfigured with fortune.
His wife resembles him, but is still a handsome woman,
She has never bound her feet or her belly.
Some of the party are his children, it seems,
And some his grandchildren;
No generation appears to intimidate another.
He is interested in people, without wanting to
    convert them or pervert them.
He eats with gusto, but not with lust;
And he drinks, but is not drunk.
He is content with his age, which has always suited him.
When he discusses a dish with the pretty waitress,
It is the dish he discusses, not the waitress.
The table-cloth is not so clean as to show indifference,
Not so dirty as to signify a lack of manners.
He proposes to pay the bill but knows he will not be
    allowed to.
He walks to the door like a man who doesn't fret
    about being respected, since he is;
A daughter or granddaughter opens the door for him,
And he thanks her.
It has been a satisfying evening. Tomorrow
Will be a satisfying morning. In between
    he will sleep satisfactorily.
I guess that for him it is peace in his time.
It would be agreeable to be this Chinese gentleman.

'WHY ISN'T YOUR POETRY MORE PERSONAL?'

Well, madam, I was never personal.
Never had the chance to be personal.
Was a poor boy who won a scholarship,
And became a case, a crisis, and
(Except that the word wasn't known
Round our way) a symbol.
Life started out on the wrong foot,
And so it continued.
At the age of sixteen I fell in love
(She was, I found out later, precocious mistress
To the Mayor's prodigal son).
I stood speechless under her bedroom —
She lived in a public house kept by her father
Who had to think of his licence —
Was rewarded with a curl of her curtain's lip
And a lot of rain.
Arrived home, as a budding symbol,
With a bad cold in the head.
And so it continued.
I won another scholarship. (Symbols
Tend to repeat themselves).
And uncles had much to say on this score,
Who might have had to keep our family.
The working class are against symbols.
I cultivated my own garden,
And it grew common or garden weeds.
Went out with an apron of wild oats,
And found the countryside already under cultivation.
I could feel symbolism creeping through my joints.
Was it contagious? My mother didn't catch it.
When doing was in order, I did too little;
When it wasn't, I did too much.

I published a poem
(And dictators never read poems)
And a dictator read it.
I began to suspect that symbols had a sense of humour.
If I mentioned art, it seemed
I was reactionary, or else was radical.
(Who else, through a hack lecture, would make *The Times?*)
I was freedom infringed, or freedom misused.
Was invited to pronounce on large topics,
But neither shot nor knighted.
I grew too big for my boots, and
Developed a corn.
Even symbols can lose heart.
Now they have given me up as a bad job —
I shall start to be personal any minute, madam.

THE OLD ADAM

(Japan, Singapore, South-East Asia)

IN THE CATALOGUE

It was a foreign horror.
A cold and lonely hour,
A place waste and littered,
And this figure standing there.

Like at first a prized
Cherry sapling swathed in straw.
It was no tree. It was enclosed
In a straw cocoon, and

Wore a hood of sacking
Over the might-be head
And the should-be shoulders.
It seemed to be looking.

What did I fear the most?
To ignore and bustle past?
To acknowledge and perhaps
Find out what best was lost?

It didn't accost. I did.
Rattling in my outstretched hand,
I hoped that money would talk,
A language of the land.

Some inner motion stirred the straw.
My stomach turned, I waited
For its — what? — its rustling claw
Or something I could not conceive.

What happened was the worst.
Nothing. Or simply, the straw
Subsided. 'Please, please!'
I begged. But nothing more.

Fear is glad to turn to anger.
I threw the money down and left,
Heedless of any danger,
Aside from vomiting.

From twenty yards I turned
To look. The shape stood still.
Another ten yards, and I strained
My eyes on icy shadows —

The shape was scrabbling for my coins!
I thanked my stomach. Then
Thanked God, who'd left the thing
Enough to make a man.

POLITICAL MEETING

Nothing human is alien to me.
Except knives, and maybe the speeches
Of politicians in flower.

Dampness, of decay and growth,
Arises all round us,
Indigenous mist from earth's two-way flow:

Can you make out which is which?
I could fall down and rot right on the spot,
Equally I could knife this orator

With all the gusto of youthful delinquency.
Except that the knife is alien to me.
One must hold on to some inhibitions —

Though I still feel the haft in my fist.
God help us, he is only talking,
His expression blurred in the general haze.

A knowing man, doing his job,
Quoting nimbly from several literatures,
Joking with his sworn professional enemies.

Laughter coughs through the mist,
Students hoot genially, a child falls
Out of a tree, bulbs and innuendoes crackle,

And solemn pressmen keep the score
(The workers, perhaps, are working).
We all behave in the manner expected of us.

Then am I pedantic, to look for knives
In the hedges and a mist of blood?
We can't make out our friends, we drift off singly.

PRIME MINISTER

Slowly he ticks off their names
On the long list:
All the young political men.

As he was once himself.
He thinks of how he despised the others
    — the a-political,
      the English-educated,
      the students he called 'white ants
In their ivory tower.'

Not so long ago, in fact,
He coined that happy phrase 'white ants'.
How he despised them, all they cared for
Was lectures, essays and a good degree!

A small thing these days
    — he tells himself —
To be arrested.
Incredulously he remembers
Not once was he arrested, somehow.

Slowly he ticks off the names
On the list to be arrested.
Tonight, isn't it? Yes,
Between 2 and 4 when the blood runs slow.
The young political men,
Full of fire, hot-blooded.
    — For a moment,
He thinks he sees his own name there.
'Red ants,' he hisses,
Thrusting the list at a waiting policeman.

MEETING THE MINISTER FOR CULTURE

— At a party.
In that borderland between
Apologetics and apology:
Neither wishing to revoke,
Neither wishing to provoke.
While tacitly agreeing
That the weather,
The latest drainage schemes,
The brand-new Parliament House,
Are hardly worthy themes.

> He talks about United Nations,
> A large and distant subject —
> In the accent of the region
> (The accent which recalls
> So many pretty girls);
> One listens to the accent
> Rather than his news
> (The accent will last longer
> Than this particular voice,
> These particular views).

Then I talk about my students,
A cultural matter.
And he prefers the past
(Before he was a Minister),
And I prefer the present
(Since I became Professor).
I can't deny his past,
He can't deny my present.
The ice we skate on
Is more than thick enough.

Then, after all,
He talks of Parliament House,
Its brand-new architecture,
A cultural matter.
Which blends the occidental
(Walls of glass)
With (horn-rimmed roofs) the oriental.
But is curiously ill-lit.
Already two have walked alas
Through its walls unwittingly.

The story takes our fancy.
Teller and listener laugh,
Each in the accent of his country.
I start an explication
Of this transparent allegory —
And then remind myself,
It's no tutorial session —
And fetch beer from the fridge.
Such warmth might melt the ice
On which we skate so nicely.

CHANGE

Times have changed.
Remember the helplessness
Of the serfs,
The inexplicable tyrannies
Of the lords.

But times have changed.
Everything is explained to us
In expert detail.
We trail the logic of our lords
Inch by inch.

The serfs devised religions,
And sad and helpful songs.
Sometimes they ran away,
There was somewhere to run to.
Times have changed.

A LIBERAL LOST

Seeing a lizard
Seize in his jaws
A haphazard moth,

With butcher's stance
Bashing its brainpan
Against the wall,

It was ever your rule
To race to the scene,
Usefully or not.

(More often losing
The lizard his meal, not
Saving the moth.)

Now no longer.
Turning away, you say:
'It is the creature's nature,

He needs his rations.'
And in addition
The sight reminds you

Of that dragon
Watching you with jaws open
(Granted, it is his nature,

He needs his rations),
And — the thing that nettles you —
Jeering at your liberal notions.

SOCIALIST-REALIST

So he composes what he must.
Memos, business letters, all the
Prose that keeps him in his post.

'I would write fiery verses,
Pity for the poor, for the oppressed
A hope, and hatred for the bosses.'

A woman visits him, whom he
(At her suggestion) once seduced,
And weeps a while, half-heartedly.

'For love the whole world cries,
Love is understanding.
My metaphors would dry their eyes.'

Rain falls like silken whips.
He must forgo his evening walk
Along the sea, past waiting ships.

'I would race out, in storm,
To storm the ironclad ministries,
My words cold steel, my body warm.'

The blood runs slow, flesh withers,
Tethered to his bones. 'I'd gladly give
My flesh and blood and bones for others!'

To strike that special tone,
Wholly truthful, intimate
And utterly unsparing,

A man communing with himself,
It seems you need to be alone,
Outwardly unhearing —

As might be now,
The streets wiped clean of traffic
By the curfew

(Apart from odd patrolling
Jeeps, which scurry through
This decent district),

The noise of killing
Far away, too distant
To be heard, above this silence

(A young Malay out strolling
— If you insist on instance —
Chopped by a Chinese gang of boys;

A party of Malays
Lopping an old man's Chinese head,
Hot in their need to burn his hut;

The riot squad,
Of some outlandish race,
Guns growing from their shoulders),

Until tomorrow's news,
And subsequent White Papers,
Analysing, blaming, praising,

Too distant to be heard
Above this heavy hush
Of pealing birds and crickets wheezing,

Tones of insects self-communing,
Birds being truthful with themselves,
Intimate and unsparing —

But birds are always chirping,
Insects rattling, always truthful,
Having little call to twist,

Who never entertained large dreams
Or made capacious claims,
Black lists or white lists:

It hardly even seems
The time for self-communing,
Better attend to nature's artists.

SMALL HOTEL

Not *Guest* —
The Chinese, those corrected souls, all know
A guest is never billed, whereas the
Essence of my aspect is, I pay —

But *Occupier*. Good words cost no more.
The Occupier is hereby kindly warned,
It is forbidden strictly by the Law
— In smudged ungainly letters on his door —
Not to introduce into this room
Prostitutes and gambling, and instruments of
Opium Smoking and spitting on the floor.

By Order, all the lot, *The Management.*
The Chinese have immense respect for Order,
They manage anything you name, except

To keep their voices down. Outside my door
The Management all night obeys the Law,
Gambles and introduces prostitutes,
And spits upon the floor and kicks around
The instruments of opium smoking.

It is forbidden to the Occupier
To sleep, or introduce into his room
Dreams, or the instruments of restoration.
He finds he has his work cut strictly out
To meet the mandates of the Law and Order.

Coffee, frying garlic and a sudden calm
Imply the onset of a working day.
Kings and queens and jacks have all departed,
Mosquitoes nurse their bloody hangovers.

So large a bill of fare, so small the bill!
A yawning boy bears off my lightweight bag,
Sins of omission make my heavier load.
Insulting gringo. Cultural-imperialist.

Maybe a liberal tip will mollify
The Law, the Order, and the Management? —
With what I leave behind on that hard bed:
Years off my life, a century of rage
And envy.

TO OLD CAVAFY, FROM A NEW COUNTRY

'Imperfect? Does anything human escape
That sentence? And after all, we get along.'

But now we have fallen on evil times,
Ours is the age of goody-goodiness.

They are planning to kill the old Adam,
Perhaps at this moment the blade is entering.

And when the old Adam has ceased to live,
What part of us but suffers a death?

The body still walks and talks,
The mind performs its mental movements.

There is no lack of younger generation
To meet the nation's needs. Skills shall abound.

They inherit all we have to offer.
Only the dead Adam is not transmissive.

They will spread their narrowness into space,
The yellow moon their whitewashed suburbs.

He died in our generation, the old Adam.
Are our children ours, who did not know him?

We go to a nearby country, for juke-boxes and
Irony. The natives mutter, 'Dirty old tourists!'

We return, and our children wrinkle their noses.
Were we as they wish, few of them would be here!

Too good for us, the evil times we have fallen on.
Our old age shall be spent in disgrace and museums.

THE ANCIENT ANTHROPOLOGIST

Let me tell you how it happened. Once
I had my finger on the pulse,
The pulse of a large and noteworthy people.

This pulse was a pile-driver, a pounder
On golden gates and coffin lids, a grinder
Of organs, a kraken, a jetstream of tears.

Believe me, it was swings and Ferris wheels,
Switchbacks and Ghost Trains and Walls
Of Death, dodgems and multifarious booths.

I dug in my heels, hung on by my nails.
Till 'Hands off!' thundered that great pulse,
Though not so great as not to notice me.

Perhaps it misconceived my fingers pressed
Concupiscently? Or set to twist its wrist?
— Activities that fall outside my field.

That was long ago. Today I'm as you find me.
All my articulations flapping freely,
Free from every prejudice, shaking all over.

POET WONDERING WHAT HE IS UP TO

— A sort of extra hunger,
Less easy to assuage than some
— Or else an extra ear

Listening for a telephone,
Which might or might not ring
In a distant room

— Or else a fear of ghosts
And fear lest ghosts might not appear,
Double superstition, double fear

— To miss and miss and miss,
And then to have, and still to know
That you must miss and miss anew

— It almost sounds like love,
Love in an early stage,
The thing you're talking of

— (but Beauty — no,
Problems of Leisure — no,
Maturity — hardly so)

— And this? Just metaphors
Describing metaphors describing — what?
The eccentric circle of your years.

UNLAWFUL ASSEMBLY

ROMAN REASONS

No wide-eyed innocent, he
Had heard tell of villainy,
Had noticed
That one's loot was one's pay.
Yet he could say
-- Seeking no comfort in numbers,
In mutuality's immunity —
'I am alone the villain of the earth.'

Finding good reasons
(Reasons are good),
Finding reasons
For the serial assassinations,
For the quotidian killings
(One's pay was one's loot),
The convenient weddings,
And the other treasons.
But not for what he had done.

Despite the logic, the prior logic,
The good, the worthy reasons,
Ratified by that old manual
He carried in his head,
Those *Hints for Roman Soldiers*,
Those counsels scratched in red —

The reasons, the decent reasons,
Each day stronger,
For his leaving their service
— An ageing general, all heart and no brain,
An ageing native woman, wrinkles and wiles —
Who couldn't be served any longer.

And yet, when it was done,
Expeditiously and quietly done —
An emperor, a Jove, a breaker of hearts,
A queen, a Venus, a breaker of hearts.
Larger than life — unfair, unfair!
From time to time men die, it would seem,
For love, and the crocodiles eat them.

Healthy, cheerful, realistic. Yet
Somehow unable to excuse himself,
Those *Hints* less lucid than he'd thought,
And logic a botched breastplate.
Alone the villain of the earth. Alone.
So, heart failure in a ditch.
Expeditiously and quietly done,
Unnoticed by *Les Nouvelles d'Egypte*
Or the Roman *Gazette,*
Their columns packed with acts and scenes —

Enobarbus, wine-bearded captain,
You are the hero of my play!

AFTER THE GODS, AFTER THE HEROES

You can see how easily a man is silenced.
Merely two or three helpers to twist his arms
Behind his back, shove him into a conveniently
Parked vehicle, drive him to a quiet place and
Beat his teeth in. Eventually he falls silent.

Don't talk about heroism. Its lifetime is a breath.
Heroes with bullets in their heads are just
Bodies. Their families are put to the expense of
Burying them. Even the quietest funeral costs money.

Opinion is informed these days. No one's readily
Excited. There have been so many heroes.
Sensibility alters from generation to generation, and
The general feeling is that people who get into trouble
Are troublesome. And the ones who fail to recover are
Born suicides.

In any case, can even the expert tell a hero from a
Villain? What are the distinguishing marks?

The history books are full already.
You can't buy space in the papers for love or money.
The papers are occupied with quintuplets, with modes,
With civil murder, with the heroism of pet dogs.
Don't adduce the inspirational power of example
But rather the dehortative authority of example.
No use talking of freedom as if it were an essential
Vegetable or a family car. You are talking to
Knowledgeable men and women, who eat vegetables, who
Own cars.

It hurts to say so, but in our time
Perhaps you will have to rely on the others, on
Paterfamilias and materfamilias, clerks bored by their
Desks, graduates with pass degrees and no special field,
Grandads out for a last fling, girls with odd fancies,
Boys who would write verse, if they could, and get it
Off their chests. . .
Those non-heroes that the poorest country's rich in.

The leaders of the masses seem to have stopped
Leading. Now you are left with the masses.
Their separate preferences and small tenacious ambitions,
Their tendency (being too many to shoot or put in prison)
To survive in private.

Either that, or else go hang yourself, and
Die in private. Leave an open letter, dignified,
Reproachful. Also, if the papers are to print it,
Irreproachable and brief.

PROCESSIONAL

(for William Walsh)

Where are they all? —
The Chancellor and the Vice-Chancellor,
The Deputy Vice-Chancellor and the Registrar,
The Bursar, the Deans of the several Faculties,
The Director of Extra-Mural Studies,
The Estate Officer and the Librarian,
The Chairman of the University Council,
The Esquire Bedell and the Public Orator?

For the scaffolding has collapsed, the
Scaffolding of the impending Science Tower,
Has collapsed, with the long thin noise of the
Crumbling of a termite-riddled ivory tower.
And underneath are two female labourers,
Sought for by their colleagues like buried and
Perishable treasure. Now a trousered leg is
Uncovered, and pulled upon, and at its end is an
Ivory visage, a whitened stage concubine's,
Slashed with a vulgar wash of red.

And where is the University Health Physician?
(He is sick, he has left, he is on sick leave.)

And first will arrive the Fire Brigade,
With their hoses and helmets and hatchets
To exhume the already exhumed. And then
The police car with its mild unworried policemen
And hypnotic radio. And last of all,
In accordance with protocol, the ambulance,
To remove whatever the firemen and the policemen
Are no longer interested in.

But where are they all? —
The Development and the Public Relations Officer
And the various Assistant Registrars,
The Vice-Dean and the Sub-Dean of Law,
The Chairman of the Senior Common Room Committee,
The Acting Head of the School of Education,
The Readers and the Senior Lecturers
(The Professors we know are all at work),
And the Presidents respectively of the Local and
The Expatriate Academic Staff Associations?
This is a bad day for an accident.

Till a clerk arrives, a clerk from the
Administration, to administer the matter.
And order is imposed and sense is made.
The scaffolding consisted of old wood left out
Too long in the monsoon rains, and the women
Took too much sand up with them, because the
Contractor told them to get a move on, since he
Was hurrying to finish the job, because. . .
And they fell through four floors,
Carrying the scaffolding with them at each floor,
The sodden planking and the bamboo poles,
And now the scaffolding and the sand and the
Labourers all lie scattered on the ground.
The day and the hour are determined, and the
Victims identified as One Science Tower
(Uncompleted) and Two Labourers, Female, Chinese,
Aged about 20 and 40 respectively,
Who also look rather incomplete.

The Chancellor and the Vice-Chancellor,
The Deputy Vice-Chancellor and the Registrar. . .
There was little occasion for them after all.

The accident has been thoroughly administered —
Moved and seconded, carried and minuted.
A gaggle of idle Assistant Lecturers tap
On their watches, seditiously timing
The ambulance. And in the distance
The fire engine's bell can be heard already.

THE MYSTERIOUS INCIDENT AT THE
ADMIRAL'S PARTY

Moored in his favourite Eastern port,
This jolly British Admiral
Must give a party on his ship,
With jolly guests, Malays, Chinese,
And Indians and English too.
Says he, 'I like the sarong well,
Trim gear, I wear it when I can.'
Good Jack, who likes Malay costume!
Approval flutters like the gulls,
Down go the drinks, up come the words.
'Although,' he says, 'it tends to slip,
It slips and slides below my hips,
It's hard to keep a sarong up.'
A Chinese lady speaks, sedate
And sweet. 'Then Admiral you need
A songkok.' Songkok as you know
Is headwear proper to sarong.
But Admiral and nearby guests,
They do not know what songkok is,
They think they hear some other words.
Some gape, some giggle and some gasp,
And jolly shaken Jack withdraws
Upon his bridge and all disperse.
This Chinese lady at a loss,
She asks her spouse in Mandarin,
But what, but why? Who, unbeknown,
Now scouts about the huddled groups.
Then joins his wife. 'Ah me, my dear,'
He murmurs in their tongue, 'To keep
His sarong up — they thought you said —
The Admiral needs a strong —'

'For shame!' in spotless Mandarin
This well-bred lady cries, 'Oh filthy-
Minded foreign hounds! Oh deep disgrace!
What can they think of Chinese dames,
These British gentlemen? Away!'
So Admiral is hurt, Malays
Offended, English persons shocked,
And Chinese lady hates the lot.
Weigh anchor, jolly Admiral —
Let drop these oriental tricks,
Be stayed with buttons and gold braid!

NEW POEMS

CHARACTER OF THE HAPPY GUERRILLA

Sure, I'm for freedom,
Without it, life's not much.
With nothing else,
Freedom's not much either.

If no lines were drawn
Who would stir his stumps?
Boundaries exclude us,
They also invite us.

Vive the small difference
Of this state from that!
Free people die of boredom,
Looking keeps us living.

> The landscape's poxed
> And patched with frontiers.
> Once I was a teacher
> Of literature;
> I failed to perceive
> That the whole of the literature of Europe
>   from Homer
> Composed a simultaneous order.
> I could only see the borders,
> The existing monuments,
> Toll gates, guard houses and gun sites,
> A landscape disordered
> By a thousand simultaneous poets.

Sure, it's a dog's life,
Being hounded;
But every dog has its day.
Keep your boots dubbined,

Sheath-knife sharp, story
In good shape, smart but not fancy.

It's not as if
There's so much competition for it,
For freedom.
There's enough to go round
If you go round looking for it.
It's usually across the border.

TAKEN PRISONER

On falling into hostile hands
It is advantageous
If you find no tongue in common

So, they are forced to strip their speech
To pidgin, or you
To guess, as is simple, at their few requirements:

Speak out. Shut up. Sit down. Stand up.
Clothes off. Clothes on. Come here. Lie there.

Saved from idiom, from innuendo
From the sounds of childhood, the words of love
The accent of the nerves, the bowels' echo

So, you can say, through the long night, waiting:
These creatures are not like us
They do not speak like us

(Much virtue out of Babel
They howl like werewolves, they grunt like Godzilla
None shall translate them)

So, you are wrapped in silence
In a tower of silence

So, you can say, as the blade is falling:
These creatures are not like us
We are —

So, you forget yourself
You are forgotten

SOMEWHERE IN ASIA

Almost the only remaining union
Almost the only remaining leftwing union
Is
The Goldsmiths and Silversmiths Union.

Craftsmen who have catered long and faithfully
To the aristocracy and the bourgeoisie
Moulding thin circles for middleclass fingers
Beating out brooches and bangles for the wrists
And breasts of the concubines of towkays
And the so-called models who consort with
Foreign capitalists.

Now on their rooftop flutter red banners
Spangled with Chinese characters
Swearing Till Death To Protect The Dignity
Of The Great Leader Chairman Mao
And swearing in different manner
At certain of the local and littler leaders.

Goldsmiths and silversmiths are anachronistic
In a city of concrete and glass and plastic
And chromium and cultured pearls —
And in one's simple and feckless way
One rather likes to think of these bespectacled old
Craftsmen in a glory of silver and gold
Swearing till death.

TOURIST PROMOTION

For the tourists, who stay in the
Large new tourist hotels, the
Chief tourist attractions are the
Other large new tourist hotels.

For the querulous and wayward
There were once the local monkeys,
Who lived in the ancient tree-tops
Long before the hotels were thought of.
The tourists enticed the monkeys down
From the trees with monkey nuts and
Breakfast rolls. And the monkeys
Scampered across the road and were
Squashed by the buses transporting
Fresh tourists to see the monkeys.
It was not a pretty sight.

So now the tourists are confined to
The tourist hotels, large and new.
They pass with the greatest of ease
From one to the other, escorted by porters
With large new umbrellas, or even through
Underground passages, air-conditioned and
Adorned with murals by local artists,
Conveying impressions of the local scene.
After all, the tourist hotels were created
Specifically for the sake of the tourists.

SHUM CHUN: THE PRECISIONS OF GOVERNMENT

Going in,
One's foreign currency declared
To the nearest dollar, more or less.
Says the gentle-faced official,
'Show me what is in your pocket' —
Another Hong Kong dollar and some cents.
'Must be precise. Amend the schedule',
She clicks her small white teeth
At a foreign plot uncovered.

Coming out,
One's foreign currency declared
To the nearest dollar, more or less,
'But shall I show you what is in my pocket?'
(That shameful dollar's-worth of cents)
The stony-faced official waves me on —
As if so large a land would stand or fall
By a foreign pocketful! —
He lifts his eyebrows in amusement.

IN THE JUNGLE

The soldier ants, the red-eyed starlings,
Go about their chores. Domestic lizards
Perpetrate their stock atrocities.
A slow hawk sweeps the sky in careful circles.
A gorged bat twitches in its sleep.

He sits at his typewriter, in this jungle,
A little man of letters, wondering
Who'll take the next bite, who'll be bitten.
It may be only fifteen hundred words
On some new travel book: to him it always
Feels like his last will and testament.

THE SENSITIVE PHILANTHROPIST

If I give you money,
Give you baksheesh,
Will you stay away
Until next week?

Since money talks
We don't need to,
Neither you to me
Nor me to you.

If I give you money
Will you make sure
That the others keep away,
Without me giving more?

Will you promise
To put to flight
All your legless colleagues
By day and by night?

If I give you money
Will you agree
To hide your stump away,
Where I can't see?

Will you state in writing
That it was done on purpose
And doesn't really hurt,
The arms, the legs, the nose?

Can't I send a cheque
Regular each week
By registered letter,
So we need never meet?

J.T. ON HIS TRAVELS

Perhaps you thought she was a child
Perhaps you thought you liked the thought

She doesn't pretend to be a virgin
Her son is lying on the only bed

Almost her size, she carries him
Still sleeping to a next-door cupboard

She brings a bucket of water back
To give herself a local wash

You feel you prefer your own french letter
Hers look secondhand

You she will wash hereafter
If you last that long

Either way you are damned—
If you manage it, for unfeelingness

If you don't, for lack of feeling
John Thomas, old Whitey, you can't win.

MEANS TEST

The top people
Receive lots of Christmas cards and large
A foot square, in purple and gold
The Ministers and the MPs
The senior servants in sensitive services
The importers and exporters and industrialists
The presidents of shipping lines
The chairmen of airlines
They receive cards at Christmas both large and many
From Embassies and High Commissions
Executives and industrialists
Presidents of shipping lines
Chairmen of airlines.

Exempli gratia, Japan Air Lines
Arrives in the form of a huge fan and
Carries an appropriate message in several languages
And the minimum of advertising and
A work of art thrown in.

Tools of the trade
The company pays.

In your father's house
They will require large mansions
In which to hang their Christmas cards.

The bottom people
Receive fewer and smaller Christmas cards
In one single language
A simple message, the price is sometimes
Marked on the back
They send fewer and smaller cards at Christmas

The bottom people pay for their Christmas cards
Out of their own pocket.

In your father's house
They will only require small mansions
In which to hang their Christmas cards
And
Since they are used to paying out of their own pocket
Your father can charge them rent.

GOODBYE EMPIRE

It had to go
So many wounded feelings
And some killings —
In a nutshell, too expensive

Though its going
Scarcely set its subjects free
For freedom —
Life still exacts a fee

In wounded feelings
And also killings
Slates wiped clean
Soon attract new chalkings

At least the old regime
Allowed its odd anomalies
Like my orphaned Irish dad
One of those Wild Geese

Who floundered over India
In the shit and out of it
Getting a stripe, and then
Falling off his horse and losing it.

MASTER KUNG AT THE KEYBOARD

(for Lee Kum Sing)

He's Oriental, he's Japanese, he's Chinese
Watch and you'll see him trip over his tail!
He's a child! What can he know of Vienna woods
Of Ludwig's deafness and J.S.B.'s fine ears?

Of tiaras and galas and programmes
Of hussars and cossacks and pogroms
Of Vespers, Valhallas and Wagrams
And the fine old flower of the Vienna woods?

(Wine, beef, pheasant, cheese, thirst, hunger)

Reared on rice and Taoist riddles
Water torture and the Yellow River
Yang Kwei-fei and one-stringed fiddles —
What can he know of the Water Music
Of barges and gondolas
Of emperors and haemophilias
Of the Abbé, the Princess, and her black cigars?

Wer das Dichten will verstehen
Muss ins Land der Dichtung gehen
Seven days with loaded Canon
Snapping prince and priest and peon.

So he went overseas for his studies? —
It is not in his blood.

What is in his blood?
Blood is.

(Rice, tea, pork, fish, hunger, thirst)

Compared with the minimum of 4,000 characters
Required at the finger-tips for near-literacy
And admission into provincial society
88 keys are child's play.

Play, child!

His heart pumps red rivers through his fingers
His hands chop Bechsteins into splinters
His breath ravishes the leaves
His hair never gets in his eyes.

I am down on my knees.

Every second pianist born is a Chinese
Schubert, Chopin, Mozart, Strauss and Liszt —
He'll be playing on
When the old Vienna woods have gone to chopsticks
Chopsticks every one.

TERMINAL

A small boy, four years
Or so of age,
And tired and confused,
In a noisy, crowded building,
His ears still hurting
From some mysterious ailment.
He trails behind his parents,
Tired too, if less confused.

Then the people all take sides,
Like in a game,
His father joins the Caucasian file,
His mother the Other.
Which team is his team?
He hears them talking,
His English father, Chinese mother,
And the man who owns the building,

Who rubs his head:
'There's this queue and there's that queue,
There isn't any third queue.
I don't know what to say!'

Neither does the little boy,
He is tired and confused.
In front of him the two queues stretch away,
There isn't any third queue.

DAUGHTERS OF EARTH

'Why are you weeping, but why are
You weeping so into your gin?'

The world, the state of the world
It makes me weep, weep into my gin

'But why weep, but why? An editor tells us
A new spirit everywhere, fresh hope astir. . .'

I continue to weep, I go on weeping
Into my gin, my rather weak gin —

I see a country where the people will vote
Vote for a government that admits the word Fuck

I see another where the people will vote
Vote for a government that excludes the word Fuck

'But why do you weep, weep into your gin
On account of a word, of merely a word?'

To permit the people to use the word Fuck
To forbid the people to use the word Fuck

For reasons arrived at, explained and agreed
For reasons arrived at, explained and agreed —

Which is why I am weeping, weep into my gin
That we live in a word-world, world only of words

And what, as the sober man said, is my portion
But gin and despair, dissipation and tears?

ROYALTIES

As 'Name of individual, partnership, or corporation to
    whom paid'
I find my own, followed by (in brackets) 'Faust'.
The amount of income received in this capacity is $3.30
    gross,
From which I am glad to see no tax has been withheld.

Egotist as he is
One had never thought the Devil so close-fisted.
He wasn't always:
Gretchen — Helen — contributions to knowledge — all that
    real estate. . .
What can have changed him?

And yet, Goethe only lasted a couple of months after
    completing his masterpiece,
So I could even be said to be lucky, nearly twenty-four years
    after publication, still making $3.30 out of a little crib
    of the Master's epic designed for non-German-speaking
    near-dropouts taking the World Literature course.

None of us, it seems, even though no tax is deducted,
    gets much for selling his soul.
The sea took back the land, Gretchen lost her head, Helen
    was incorporeal, the scholarship soon discredited;
Faust died the moment he started to enjoy life, and Goethe's
    poetry is supplanted by a crib —
It was always a buyer's market, always.

MORE MEMORIES OF UNDERDEVELOPMENT

'God's most deep decree
Bitter would have me taste: my taste was me.'

A lapsed Wesleyan, one who dropped out
Halfway through the Wolf Cubs, and later ran howling
From Lourdes by the first bus back, whose idea of
High wit is 'God si Love', who would promptly
Ascribe the sight of Proteus rising from the sea
To spray in the eyes or alcohol in the brain —
Yet these words appal me with recognition,
They grow continuously in terror.

So how much more must they mean
To these young though ageless Catholics, to whom I am
Rashly expounding Father Hopkins!

But no,
They seem to find it a pleasing proposition,
The girls are thinking how nice they taste, like moon-cake
Or crystallised pears from Peking,
The boys are thinking how good they taste, like crispy noodles
Or bird's-nest soup.

The poor old teacher is muttering curses,
Four letters cut to three out of care for his job:
Was I born to bring a sense of sin among you,
You oriental papists! Obviously Rome was not built in
Three hundred years. A lurching humanist,
Is it for me to instruct you in the fall complete?

Their prudent noses wrinkle almost imperceptibly.
Oh yes, they tell themselves, the poor old man,
His taste is certainly him. . .
And they turn to their nicer thoughts,
Of salted mangoes, pickled plums, and bamboo shoots,
And scarlet chillies, and rice as white as snow.

TO A WAR POET, ON TEACHING HIM
IN A NEW COUNTRY

They talk about you as if you were alive —
To hear their comments and profit thereby.
A compliment of a sort,

Though some of them think you frivolous
To stick a poppy behind your military ear,
And others complain of excessive sarcasm —
You are cynical about the war

(A suspicion persists, *re* those poppies,
That you were playing around with narcotics,
Perhaps to help you drop off again.
Court Poetic for you, my man,
Ten days confined to Lyrics. . .)

Worse, you are cynical about your mates,
Preferring rats to people, even 'haughty athletes'.
So much for Western humanism! And their Olympics!

While some find you equally unkind to the rat.
You accuse it of 'cosmopolitan sympathies'
And a paucity of proper rathood,
And you threaten to have it shot.

Practically all of them object to your attitude
Of boredom. 'The same old druid Time as ever,'
You mutter as you yawn across the parapet.
Poets are allowed to be boring,
But not to be bored —

Least of all when war is the question.
For these young people (government bursars,
Bonds to the whims of the Public Service Commission)

129

Have strong feelings on the subject of war,
An event which occurred between 1914 and 1918
In Europe.
They are very much against it,
You will be pleased to hear.

BOARD OF SELECTION

No, it is not easy to effect an
Appointment in English literature.
The chairman of the board is worrying over
Last year's riots (the bodies were traced
By the smell . . .) and next year's budget
(The British are pulling out. . . but leaving
Their literature behind them).

The dean of the faculty is an
Economist of repute and utility.
But what is the difference, he asks,
Between prose and poetry?
The candidate proposes adroitly that
Poetry is more economical than prose,
Viz., it says as much in half the space.

The economist is not satisfied.
In half the space, he muses . . . but
It takes him four times as long to understand
A piece of poetry as a piece of prose —
Which means . . .

The board make hasty calculations . . .
Which means that poetry is a false economy,
More haste, less speed.
The chairman remembers he has to build a nation
By the end of the month.

Neither I nor the candidate dare ask the
Esteemed economist which particular piece of
Poetry has so discomfited him.
It would probably have to do with daffodils
And this is an orchid-exporting country.

We submit that quite a lot of literature is
Prose and prose is pertinent to the economy.

A business man wants to know when the
Middle Ages stopped and the Renaissance started.
No one is sure. The director of education
Asks why there is so much sex in modern literature.
Because, the candidate ventures, there is so much
In modern life (excluding the English Department).
The chairman is brooding over the birth-rate.

Finally, after a disgruntled pilgrimage to
Canterbury and a brief stopover in 1984,
It is recommended that the candidate be offered
A temporary assistant lectureship at the bottom
Of the scale, subject to the survival of the
Economy, the nation, the university, the department,
And her hopes of completing her master's degree.

IMITATION OF AN ACTION

Figures shadowy to others —
To each other sharp and heavy,
In a quiet corner, dimly lighted.
The blood flows quietly;
In semi-dark, the spirit's flesh
Is carved and diced and eaten.

Is it apt for print to rant,
Late and safely distant?
Shouldn't it flow quietly
    too, and thickly,
With now and then a glint?

We sit in the court-room's blaze,
Bright imitations cram our watering eyes.

ALONG THE RIVER

They had pulled her out of the river. She was dead,
Lying against the rhododendrons sewn with spider's thread.
An oldish woman, in a shabby dress, a straggling stocking,
A worn, despairing face. How could the old do such a thing?

Now forty years have passed. Again I recall that poor
Thing laid along the River Leam, and I look once more.

They have pulled her out of the river. She is dead,
Lying against the rhododendrons sewn with spider's thread.
A youngish woman, in a sodden dress, a straggling stocking,
A sad, appealing face. How can the young do such a thing?

FASHION FIT

We are practised and perfect
In the day of telegrams and excuses.
The typist invites us to letters,
The telephone squats at our side
Like a grinning memento of life.
It punctuates our sentence, it rhymes
Through the times of the week.

The bosses are just.
We die of pleasant vices
As efficiently as possible. We kick
The wastepaper basket. Triteness
Is all. We are signed for, and folded
Away, we are laid in filing cabinets.

We have our victories.
There comes a translation of *Beowulf*
Anew in paperback. There is the stir
Of new novels, gone to new worlds
Of fellatio and the mysteries of
Sodomy. The smoke-room story
Is lost to smokers, is become an
Epiphany. We are intimate in cinemas.
And in the comfortable countries
Students are inventing unease
And disposable woes.

A CHASM IN THE CLASSROOM

'Faustus is dissatisfied, he wants
To be a god. This makes him human,
We identify with ease'

Why, this is hell,
Which way I fly

'More relevant than small Macbeth
Or senile Lear. There is no blame —
We too aspire, and rightly so'

I wished to be a man. It did not
Make me godlike. There is no blame

'To wall all Germany with brass, or
Trick the students out with silken tights —
Mere symbols of a natural drive'

Which way I drive is hell,
Nor brass nor silk keeps in or out

'The theme is existential, here and
Now — unlike the plight of Antony
The ladies' king, or clown Sir Epicure'

Why, here and now is hell,
I cannot but remember

'We each desire to be a god. The
Weaknesses are where the poetry is —
For surely hell's for other people'

One more bare hour. Which way I fly
The stars stand still, time's stopped.
I beg to differ, not dissuade.

ONE ACT

Behold
The frightful discoverer of morality

Let's take that again —
See
The discoverer of the frightful discovery
Of mortality (as the grimfaced poet put it)

For which you will receive no medal
No writeup in the National Ethical Magazine
No stiffnecked peak named after you
Nor sombre valley or newfound straits

It was there all the time
You are no more than a frightful rediscoverer
Only the fright is truly yours

('Stated thus simply, the theme may seem
Commonplace.' Served only to discover sights of
Triteness)

Hence the event requires a light and even
Humorous treatment. You might stagger away
From an unseen sword, clutching your breast
Murmuring 'Touché', and fall in the doorway
With a careless last word or two —
Like, 'I am the deed's creature'
(Though of course you are not dead
You will have to go on using words for years)

Cars hoot, the market continues to
Rise and fall, like girls' skirts
The busy persist in their diverse business

Barefaced, the dogs splay their hideous
Rears and shit on the pavements

On you too if you lie there still
Whatever ran you down — for that
There is no compensation
Nor for the bloodless gash of the
Abominable dog who at last discovered you

As so often, it would seem wiser
To play it quietly, quietly
To rise, brush your coat and walk quickly away
Your frightful discovery concealed about your person.

A month much like any other
There were five weekends in it
And no printing strike, but a rape
In Viet Nam (I believe it was), a
Symbolical German dentist removing teeth
And illusions, and a Jewish Italian
Afflicted with accidie in an elegant style
(Or maybe that was the month before)
W. Pater wrote letters to an oriental maiden
Raped by GIs, while a bored Italian Jew
Discovered the source of eternal energy in
The Antarctic (Prix des Libraires) which was
Discovered a week later by a Swede in a
Documentary novel and a balloon. A number of
Quaint peasants murdered their husbands or
Wives etc. and got off scot-free because they
Were life-enhancing. And I forgot my name
(It was found at the bottom of a page)
I wrote elegant letters to an asian woman
Murdered by the foreign soldiery. Shakespeare
Turned up, with an apt word for everything
Especially titles. I forgot my title
(The postman brought me proofs of existence)
Much drinking of *vins de pays* went on. I can
Remember a hangover. And lots of sex
In a lost world at the bottom of the Antarctic
Discovered by E. Pound, an American balloonist
And I lost my memory for several days, but
Found it at the bottom of a cheque. In a
Spare hour I tried to write a poem on life and
Death in a Vietnamese hamlet called SW18
Ravaged by peace and the brutal schoolchildren

W. Pater came about the cooker
At some stage an exhaustive life of E. Pound
Appeared. A peasant named Confucius was raped
By the brutal intelligentsia. A large man came
About the rates, a book came about the rapes, a
Large book came about Shakespeare from Voltaire
To Ungaretti. An index slipped, trouble with
An appendix, my teeth hurt. At one point (I am
Almost sure) a book reviewer died at his desk
Whose name will be found at the bottom

ANOTHER PERSON ONE WOULD LIKE TO BE

Is a 19th-century composer of
Masses for the Dead.
God knows, one has the emotions anyway
One might as well believe in them.

No call to concoct a plot
No need to write the words
No lack of occasion —
There are masses of dead.

Once I wished I were an old Chinese gentleman
Glimpsed in a Chinese restaurant
Amid masses of Chinese relatives —
With the years one's ambitions grow humbler.